STEP TWO

You Are Not Alone

First published May, 1982

Printed in the United States of America.

The following is an adaptation of one of the Twelve Steps in the program of Overeaters Anonymous. It is one person's interpretation and does not speak for the O.A. organization.

Willing to believe

When we come into the program of Overeaters Anonymous, some of us come without any belief in a Power greater than ourselves. Some of us come with very strong religious convictions. Some of us are not sure. We start wherever we are — atheist, theist, agnostic, or points in between. All that is required for O.A. membership is a desire to stop overeating. Recommended is an open mind and an attitude of willingness.

Nobody *has* to do anything in O.A. The Steps are merely suggested. They outline a process that has worked for millions of addicted people, whether the problem is drugs, alcohol, food, gambling, whatever.

If you have trouble with the idea of God as a Higher Power, relax. Don't push it. A Higher Power for you might be the strength of the group, the strength that comes from other people who have found a solution. In taking Step One you admitted that you could not manage what you ate by yourself. Step Two is a growing belief that some force greater than your efforts will provide the strength you need. At the beginning, all that is suggested is an open mind and the willingness to believe in something more powerful than your own efforts. If you have declared bankruptcy and given up on the unsuccessful methods you have been using to try to control compulsive overeating, then Step Two is really the only solution, outside of complete despair.

For most of us, seeing is believing. So our willingness to believe grows as we attend meetings and meet people who are recovering. Nothing is more convincing than to hear someone describe what they were like when they were overeating and what happened to them as a result of abstinence and the Twelve Steps. We identify with people who have the same problems we do. Their stories strike an inner chord, and we begin to think that if they found help from a Higher Power, we may too.

 ## What have you got to lose?

One thing we stand to lose by taking Step Two is the illusion of ourselves as the center of the universe. This may not be a bad idea to get rid of! When push comes to shove, do you really acknowledge any kind of force which is higher than and beyond your own ego? More than acknowledging the possibility, do you defer to such a Power in the routine situations of your everyday life? Or do you feel that a Higher Power, if indeed one exists, could not possibly be bothered by your petty concerns?

Part of our reluctance to believe may be because we do not care to recognize anything greater than our own subjectivity. The ego would like to have supreme control, whatever the situation. Who wants to play a subservient role? The world

4

encourages us to think in terms of "me first," and our psychological conditioning may make it very hard to get beyond our own intelligence and desires. If there is a Power greater than ourselves, we are neither the master of our fate nor the captain of our souls. Ouch, that hurts.

On the other hand, by getting rid of egotistical illusions, we become better able to live life. For one thing, we no longer have to try to maintain a pretense of self-sufficiency. We can ask for help. We can begin to have faith in a spiritual Power that will make us well.

Another thing you are likely to lose by taking Step Two (and continuing on with the others) is excess weight. Most of us come to the program in order to get thin, look terrific, and live happily ever after. When we lose the weight, however, most of us discover that we still have the same *living* problems we did when we were fat. In order to find a way to cope with those problems without going back to using food as a crutch and regaining all the weight, it is our experience that we have to work the Steps. We come to O.A. in order to get thin, and we stay for the program. But we do lose weight, and that is very nice.

A great deal of fear is something that also seems to get lost as we progress through the Steps. By coming to believe in a Higher Power that *does* care about everything that happens to us, we can give up more and more of our old anxieties. Some of us have a sensation of having "come home" with the very first meeting we attend. Somehow we know that at last we are where we belong. There is an answer; there is a solution. Kindred spirits are experiencing it, and so can we. What we cannot do alone will be done for us by the strength found in the group.

Fear, self-centered pride, loneliness and isolation, resentments, anger, insecurity, hopelessness — we stand to lose varying amounts of all of these negative characteristics along with varying amounts of excess pounds. When we begin to believe that a Higher Power can restore us to sanity, anything can happen.

Who's insane?

"Not me. I eat too much, but I'm certainly not insane. Crazy about food, maybe, but not crazy." Some of us need quite a bit of time in the program before we see just how far from sanity we were when we walked into the first meeting. We may realize our previous insanity gradually, or it may come to us in a series of sudden flashes or insight.

To begin with, most of us will readily admit to using poor judgment with regard to food and eating. We may already be convinced that the way we eat is quite irrational, if not completely crazy. Closet eating, binge eating, spending more than we can afford for food, endangering health by overeating — these are all indications that our behavior, when it comes to food, is not very sane. Since being sane means being healthy, practicing unhealthy eating habits is certainly not a sane thing to do.

Realizing the insanity in other areas of our life may take a bit more time, but we eventually begin to see how interrelated it all is. The constant preoccupation with food and eating, the guilt and remorse after a binge, the fear of suffering because of one's inadequacies — these are all part of the insanity. So are withdrawal from those around us and feelings of depression. We get so used to the cycle of overeating, feeling bad, eating more to feel better, and feeling worse that we come to accept it as normal. It is only after a period of abstinence when we are on the way to recovery that we begin to see just how sick we really were.

We become aware of how we adjusted our life to support and facilitate our overeating habit. We gradually see how it affected our relationships with family and friends, job performance, school work, what we did with spare time (if there was any left over after eating), and emotional state. And yes, our spiritual state, too.

Another element in the insanity of compulsive overeating is fantasy. What do you think about when you are bingeing? Chances are your thoughts are not very firmly anchored in the real world. Anger and resentment can trigger fantasies of vengeance, of winning, of being "top dog." When we eat to escape reality, we often accompany the eating with fantasies of wish fulfillment. For a little while we pretend that everything is lovely; dreams come true, until the pain of overeating brings us back to face the here and now, and we have to go out to the store for more food, since we "ate the whole thing" and there is nothing left for anyone else.

When we are bingeing, especially on refined sugars and carbohydrates, our mental processes get dulled, to say the least, if not completely out of whack. We are not in our right minds. We say things we don't mean, and we do things we would not do if our perceptions were not so distorted with excess calories. The mental compulsion to continue to eat food which we do not physically need is itself a form of insanity.

Being restored

To be *restored* to sanity implies that sanity is our natural state. What is abnormal is the insanity that goes along with compulsive overeating. How do we come to believe that we were meant to be sane and not obsessed with food? This is where a Higher Power comes into the picture. Again, we need an open mind. As faith grows, we become convinced of a basic principle of goodness and health which is more powerful than any disease or distortion of the way we were meant to be. Working the program opens us to that source of health and wholeness. For most of us, the Power which is greater than ourselves is a loving God, as we understand the idea of God.

We do not have to subscribe to any religious creed or dogma. Our individual interpretations of God can cover a wide range of diversity. Someone who previously had not believed in God decided that he would imagine all the characteristics he would want God to have and think of Him in those terms. He thought of God as being able to give him good things, help when he needed it, and health. Furthermore, he thought of God as *wanting* to give him these gifts, as loving him, approving of him, and wanting him to be well.

A belief in the fundamental goodness of the universe is something you may not have when you come to O.A. Goodness for other people, maybe, but goodness for you, doubtful. You may have such a low opinion of yourself and so much guilt, that you feel you do not deserve goodness from a

Higher Power. As a compulsive overeater, you may have been locked inside your disease for so long that you have lost hope of being rescued or finding a way out.

Many of us have felt this way but can affirm that we did find a way out. One phrase we heard in the meeting rooms was "Keep coming back." We did. We kept going back to meetings, sometimes one every day if we were lucky enough to live in an area where daily meetings were available. Some of us went to open Alcoholics Anonymous meetings to reinforce what we were learning about the Steps and to learn more. (In the process, some of us came to realize that we were alcoholics, too, as well as compulsive overeaters.) We got a sponsor, if we didn't already have one, and we began to work the program.

Being restored involves action. We act our way into right thinking, not the other way around. It is our experience that belief comes as we act, following the directions of the program. At the beginning we need only be open to the idea that there is something bigger than self. Our belief grows as we act and as our lives are changed.

"Came to believe"

Some of us "came to" before we came to believe. We "came to" the fact that we were killing ourselves with food and hurting the people we loved with our negative emotions. "Coming to" can happen in a quick flash of insight. Coming to believe may take longer.

Even those of us who considered ourselves devout and committed to a religious faith will probably decide that we were agnostic with regard to the application of that faith, since we continued to overeat compulsively. We thought we believed in God, but we didn't apply the belief to the problem that was destroying us.

None of the Twelve Steps are taken once and for all. They were set down by the first members of A.A. who tried to describe the process they had gone through which resulted in sobriety and a spiritual awakening. The Steps are a guide. They do not necessarily happen in the same order to everyone. Most of us go back to each one again and again as the need arises and as we are prompted by outer circumstances and an inner voice. Step Two, along with the other Steps, is something we can experience many times, frequently with an increasing depth of perception.

Action reinforces belief, and belief in turn supports action. As you look back over your life from the vantage point of abstinence and sanity, you may see that you now are learning what some part of you always knew about God but was afraid to believe. It is self-centered fear that makes us slow to believe. Once we get into the program and have friends we can talk to, some of this fear begins to dissipate. As we take action, faith grows.

Compulsive overeaters usually want everything to happen right away, if not yesterday. We want it all this very minute. If belief is faltering now, we may impatiently decide that it is an impossibility. "Easy does it" is one of the many useful slogans of the program. One day at a time, one meal at a time, one Step at a time. Coming to believe may not happen overnight, but that does not mean it won't happen.

We come to believe as we hear other people talk about how they have come to believe. This program is something we "catch" through exposure to those who are living it. The fear which hampers our belief is based on pride, selfishness, and isolation. Sharing our fears and revealing our vulnerability to understanding, supportive people goes a long way toward replacing the fears with faith. "This is how it worked for me. You can do it, too. I know you can. I'll help you."

We see the program working. We hear friends tell how a Higher Power has given them abstinence and is removing their desire to overeat. They declare that they could never do this by themselves. They give examples of how this Higher Power is working out other problems in their lives. They tell us what they were like before, what happened, and what they are like now. We come to believe that a Higher Power can restore us, too, to sanity.

But often we come to believe gradually. Two years from now, when you look back at today, you will probably be amazed at how far you have come.

"I prayed and nothing happened"

"I believed in God once. Sometimes I still do. But I have prayed and prayed that I would be able to eat less and lose weight, and it hasn't worked. So it's hard for me to believe, much as I'd like to."

At one time or another, most compulsive overeaters have probably prayed for control. When control does not come, it's easy to give up on God. Fortunately, God does not give up on us. If you have read this far, you undoubtedly have at least a small hope that the O.A. program will be the solution you have been searching for. That hope requires a plan of concrete action and the support of other people in order to bear fruit.

It is our experience that prayer by itself is not enough. There are things we need to do. Writing down a food plan and calling it in to a sponsor commits us more firmly to carrying out our good intentions just for today. It may be hard for you to pick up the phone and ask someone else for help. It is hard for most of us. We like to think we can solve our problems and manage our lives by ourselves, but we admitted in Step One that we cannot.

If we do not follow the food plan today, we may be ashamed to call tomorrow and report failure. This program requires the humility to acknowledge that we are not perfect and the faith to believe that we are learning. There are no failures, only slow successes. We may have to try many, many times before we are ready for abstinence. If your sponsor is not patient, get another sponsor. God is patient.

Use the tools of recovery that the program offers. A quiet time at the beginning of the day, part of which is spent reading the literature that is available for O.A. and A.A., becomes a daily routine that starts us off in the right frame of mind.

Going to meetings regularly and making phone calls during the day keep us on the track. Before you take that first compulsive bite, use the telephone. Write before you eat. Our Higher Power gives us abstinence and restores us to sanity, but we have to do the footwork. We are not supposed to just sit back and wait for the miracle to happen. We can't do it without help from a Higher Power, but getting the help and having our prayers answered requires our cooperation.

You are not alone

Before, when you were trying to escape from the insanity of compulsive overeating, you were probably trying to do it alone. When that didn't work, you may have joined a diet club for a period of time. Diet clubs may be very helpful for some people, but for a true compulsive overeater, more is necessary for recovery than diet alone. Most of us are well aware of what and how much we should eat. The problem is putting our knowledge into practice. Until we go beyond diet and food and begin to remove the roadblocks to emotional and spiritual growth, we will not find the strength to resist the compulsion to overeat.

As established in Step One, it is not in our power to remove the compulsion. We agree that probably no human power could do it. We came to believe "that God could and would if He were sought."

Looking back from the vantage point of the program, you may come to believe that a Higher Power was taking care of you all along. This Power, greater than yourself and your compulsion, kept you from killing yourself either with food or out of despair and led you to a group of people who have found an answer. You don't have to struggle by yourself any longer. You have friends who understand you and who need your support and help as much as you need theirs.

You are not weird or beyond hope. Your problems are not unique. When you were growing up, there may not have been anyone whom you could talk to about your fears, hopes, embarrassments, feelings of inadequacy. So you kept all of these feelings hidden, and you turned to food to ease the pain. Food may have provided temporary comfort, but it did not solve any of the problems. By keeping them to yourself and trying to ignore them by burying them in a mound of food, you cheated yourself out of valuable emotional growth. Whenever we avoid facing an uncomfortable feeling or situation, it looms even larger and more food is required to cover it up.

Turning to excess food (or to alcohol or other drugs) in order to escape the problems of living means that we inhibit emotional and spiritual development. To start growing again, we have to begin to face the problems and painful feelings rather than continue to avoid them. Some people estimate that they had an emotional age of about twelve or thirteen when they came into the program, because that was their chronological age when they stopped dealing with life and habitually numbed their feelings with food.

When the anesthetic is removed — i.e., when you limit your food intake to the amount and quality necessary to

14

maintain health, the buried pain is likely to surface. You are embarking on an exciting adventure — the discovery of who you really are and how you really feel! Even though it is exciting, it may hurt for a while. If the feelings had not been painful, there would have been no need to suppress them by overeating.

You are not alone in this adventure. There are other people who have been over a similar path and who can point out pitfalls and give encouragement. An O.A. group is especially supportive, because we identify with each other. It is an unthreatening atmosphere, one of caring and sharing. No one has to do anything he or she is not ready to do; you progress at your own pace.

When you feel an uncontrollable craving and are ready to throw abstinence and your food plan into the nearest wastebasket, you can call someone on the phone *before* you opt for self-destruction. Talking it out with a friend who understands can shed light on what you are really feeling. Maybe you are hungry, but maybe the hunger is for something other than food. Maybe you are not hungry at all, but you are using hunger to mask deep feelings of anger which you are afraid to recognize. If you eat a dozen doughnuts you will end up feeling angry, but it will be anger turned aganist yourself for eating the doughnuts, and you may never know the real reason for the anger.

Often we have been deluding ourselves for so long that without help we cannot sort out our true feelings. There is help. We do not have to keep on trying to "go it alone." The Higher Power that restores us to sanity frequently works through other people.

Sanity

Webster's dictionary defines compulsion as "an irresistible impulse to perform an irrational act." The compulsive overeater puts more and more food into his or her mouth, not because of physical need but because of the inability to stop eating. To be restored to sanity includes being able to eat a measured amount of food every day and then being able to stop eating and go on to do something else.

In O.A., part of becoming sane again involves specific actions with regard to food. Since we are powerless over it, we need some outside form of control. It is a Higher Power that removes the obsession and gives us abstinence. What we do is decide on a daily food plan and work with a qualified sponsor.

Irrational, "spontaneous" eating on impulse has been the cause of a great deal of misery for most of us. One of the ways we eliminate this irrational eating is to know exactly what we are going to have for each meal each day. The plan will vary according to individual requirements and the advice of one's doctor. By writing down a plan and calling it in to a sponsor, we can let go of the mental obsession with what we are going to eat, one day at a time.

It is insanity for an alcoholic to take the first drink when past experience indicates that the first drink will inevitably lead to getting drunk. In the same way, it is insanity for a compulsive overeater to take the first compulsive bite, when experience has proved over and over again that the first compulsive bite inevitably leads to a binge. Being restored to sanity means that we will stop kidding ourselves that this time it will be different. When we are sane, we know that we have an illness which cannot be cured but which can be controlled by abstinence and the Twelve Steps. We know that the first compulsive bite will eventually become a binge. No matter how thin we are or how long we have been in the program, we remain compulsive overeaters. For us, snacks and between-meal nibbling are insane, since they trigger the obsession, and sooner or later (usually sooner) we are right back into uncontrolled eating.

Working the Steps of this program results in a new attitude of humility, which is also part of sanity for a compulsive overeater. The ego trips of the past invariably got us into trouble. Ego trips and binges often went hand in hand and removed us farther and farther from reality.

Our past insanity probably included wide swings of mood. We were either the greatest or the worst, fantastic or hopeless. Sanity puts us in a comfortable place where we can accept ourselves as people with strengths and weaknesses, not perfect but learning.

Sanity means living in the real world instead of in a fantasy. Daydreaming of all of the marvelous things that will happen to you when you are thin, and eating while you daydream, is living in a crazy world. So is the habit of mentally rearranging circumstances to suit yourself. In this program we pray for the sanity to accept the things we cannot change; we stop trying to wish them away or eat them away. The courage to change what we can and the wisdom to know the difference are also part of the sanity which is given back to us by a Higher Power who does not intend that we should be obsessed with eating.

"Greater than ourselves"

Surrender and humility are crucial to all of the Steps. As long as we are caught up in self-centered pride, we cannot ask for help. As long as we think of ourselves as the center of the universe, there is no room for a Higher Power. If we insist on continuing to muddle through, "controlling" what we eat "our way," the illness gets worse. Compulsive overeating is a progressive disease which is physical, emotional, and spiritual. Similar to recovering alcoholics, those whose disease has been successfully arrested describe what has happened to them in terms of a "spiritual awakening." By means of spiritual growth, the compulsion to overeat was removed.

You may feel at this point that a spiritual awakening is low on your list of priorities, that all you want to do is stop overeating and lose weight, never mind the spirituality. That's what most of us wanted. Most of us found, however, that nothing worked until we stopped relying on material solutions and became willing to grow spiritually. The alternatives are fairly clear-cut: spiritual growth or physical destruction. Which do you choose?

How the spiritual awakening is experienced varies from person to person. Stories in the "Big Book"* of Alcoholics Anonymous and in the book *Overeaters Anonymous*** run the

---

* *Alcoholics Anonymous,* published by A.A. World Services, New York, NY. Available through Hazelden Educational Materials.

** Published by O.A. World Service Office, Torrance, CA. Also available through Hazelden.

gamut from dramatic moments of illumination to a slow process of gradually developing faith. What is agreed on is that a Power greater than the individual has effected a change. And that's what we are after in the first place, isn't it? A change in behavior so that we are no longer controlled by the compulsion to overeat.

We may not understand how the spiritual Power works. One doesn't have to understand how electricity works in order to use it. The Higher Power of our understanding may be anything from a vague idea of a spirit that infuses the group to a Supreme Being as described in a particular religious creed. Whatever it is, it is greater than our individual selves and does for us what we cannot do alone: It removes the compulsion to overeat and restores us to useful, fulfilling, and happy lives.